Texting

Learn How To Attract, Persuade & Seduce Anyone With Text Messages

(Sexting Tips For Dating, Romance And Relationships For Men And Women)

Judy Flannery

Published By **Elena Holly**

Judy Flannery

Texting: Learn How To Attract, Persuade & Seduce Anyone with Text Messages (SEXTING TIPS FOR dating, ROMANCE AND RELATIONSHIPS for men and women)

ISBN   978-1-77485-540-9

No part of this guidebook shall be reproduced in any form without permission in writing from the publisher except in the case of brief quotations embodied in critical articles or reviews.

Legal & Disclaimer

The information contained in this ebook is not designed to replace or take the place of any form of medicine or professional medical advice. The information in this ebook has been provided for educational & entertainment purposes only.

The information contained in this book has been compiled from sources deemed reliable, and it is accurate to the best of the Author's knowledge; however, the Author cannot guarantee its accuracy and validity and cannot be held liable for any errors or omissions.

Changes are periodically made to this book. You must consult your doctor or get professional medical advice before using any of the suggested remedies, techniques, or information in this book.

Upon using the information contained in this book, you agree to hold harmless the Author from and against any damages, costs, and expenses, including any legal fees potentially resulting from the application of any of the information provided by this guide. This disclaimer applies to any damages or injury caused by the use and application, whether directly or indirectly, of any advice or information presented, whether for breach of contract, tort, negligence, personal injury, criminal intent, or under any other cause of action.

TABLE OF CONTENTS

Chapter 1: The Basics

Let's get this party going:

The first thing to do is make sure that you've got this girl's number, and you'll call her and send her your first message. Do not worry over trying to please her. The most important thing to remember is that you don't have anything to show anybody... you're fantastic. You're a snoot. Your life is wonderful. You're always engaged in something enjoyable and exciting , and lots of girls would like to be part of your life... This is the perspective you should consider to be successful. If you approach this seeking acceptance or approval you will see it from a distance and throw you away as a squatter, I guarantee it.

What you should know about women

right from the first text you send is that women always look for a man highly valued. It's a good thing you're looking for.

Imagine going shopping with a man... it is normal to go through the door and pick up the things you require pretty quickly, don't you think? You then leave. It's simple and easy.

Have you ever had a conversation with a woman who is shopping? She reviews all the items and is looking for the best price and considers the finer points and the best. This is the way women are. When you text messages to her, they should be in the context in which you are the boss and the one she's lucky to text with. It's not meant to be an arrogant prick. It is merely a sign that you're an alpha male...act as one when you write your text messages.

The Correct Amount of Cocky

Texting is the best spot to get flirty. But being cocky on your own isn't enough. Being all confident could cause her to believe that you're the most pompous and rude person she's ever met. This is why you should be a bit cocky and humorous. Combine it with humour. Do not take yourself too seriously However, you must make it clear that you are the king of your castle.

You must be confident and amusing. Being cocky by yourself can help her to not respond to your messages however being funny and cocky is a winning combination. This kind of personality is what will make women smile and be amazed while at the same time.

Humor and humor to charm her

Important issues should be discussed in person, except if you are physically separated from one another. Make sure to keep your messages to her fun and pleasant. Being able to communicate with her with a ability to laugh is essential however, you must ensure that you're able to convey it in a way that's enjoyable.

Always remember: A lady will not forget the man who made her laugh.

Why?

It means that, despite the harsh world the man is able to make her feel happy.

How Fast Should You Respond

Ideally, you shouldn't respond too quickly, except the time it is needed or advantageous. Avoid the mistake of not allowing yourself to respond. Actually, you should not answer to any of her messages. This is a holy men's admonition: Don't make yourself available. Give her the time to forget youand then become more and more distant from you. If you're at hand every time she presses a button on her phone, there's no reason for not being there for her. It will appear as if you have no important things to accomplish. No work? No obligation? No life? This is not a positive image.

How often should you text Her

It's all about how well she responses in your text messages. If you believe that she is also interested in conversing with you, and responds to your messages so well that she asks questions and offers suggestions to keep the conversation and you are able to send her a text as often as you'd like. However, if she responds to your text messages by saying "Yes." (or "No." This is an indication that she's not interested in communicating with you. As a male it is your responsibility to be respectful of this. However, this scenario could be altered. It is important to understand her.

What is the reason she's not talking to you? Maybe you've wrote her a boring email? What do you do now?

Find out what she is interested in.

Why?

Since she might not be keen on texting with you, but if she is genuinely interested in the subject in the discussion, she may offer an alternative For instance, if she's looking to write novels, you could talk about your favourite author or inquire what novels she creates. Perhaps she will even allow you to go through her latest novel.

Consider what she'll gain from talking with you. Keep in mind it is form of communication that is two-way. It's a giving and take method.

If she truly does not want to speak and

isn't interested in talking, allow her to be. There is no need to push her. This only means she's not the woman you want to be with.

Chapter 2: What To Do And Don'ts Of Sexting

THE DO'S AND DONT'S OF Sexting
Here are some tips for sexting techniques which we've learned to will yield the most effective results. Keep in mind that you're trying to draw your Large Hairy One out of his normal habitat in your Man Cave to your love chamber. Therefore, we begin slowly and gradually acquaint him to begin with a few phrases about love, and gradually progress to a full conversation that is educational and enlightening for both of you!

When he comes out of the solitary Man Cave, blinking and falling, into the joy that is love thoughts could help him become accustomed to adult conversations in texts that go further and deeper that "k" as well as "kk" as well as "ugh"!

Make sure to time your text for Maximum Impact

Choose the ideal moment to begin your sext marketing campaign. The sext message of love that you'll drop on his head is most effective when you're in the gym or driving to home, so that he has enough time to consider it and then respond to it, not at the beginning of the day when the work is on and the message gets lost in the day's work.

Do talk straight without sarcasm

Jokes and sarcasm can become lost in the speed of the text . it's hard to convey a calm tone when you're blasting out messages with your swift thumbs. It is best to keep the more sarcastic jokes (if you are a fan of that) for times when you're with your partner so that you can have instant exchange.

Do understand that Guys are Hunters and women are gatherers

Because it is the nature of man to seek out prey, allow him chase you. Create a game in which you have to make him guess what you're wearing (and it can become fun-sexy quickly) and then you discover which of his turn-ons he is.

Do Give Him Some Attention

Everyone needs to be acknowledged. Every now and then, make use of his unique name in a textand he'll get up off the couch and feel like you are paying attention. If not, "dude" or "turkeyneck" is acceptable until he realizes the distinction between others and is therefore Worthy. If there is no special name, there's another issue to discuss!

Do fuel your imagination with Limits

You should let him know that you're open to friendly offers, but you are not for sale (or to be taken away until you've explained to him how much you appreciate it). Setting some gentle guidelines regarding the use of language can protect both sides from negative feelings. Certain words might be offensive to you and others that could make you feel. It's the same for men. (In our experiences, they aren't thrilled when they hear their male organs having been described "like penis, but it's smaller").

Do ask him what he wants.

"Tell me what you think" could be the blockade to conversations with males. However "tell me what you'd like to hear" could be the key to opening the key to receiving some honest feedback. The more comfortable you become in communicating your desire and fantasy and desires, the more you'll discover what draws him in.

To play ... Try to get Your Motor Ready, To Go The Distance

In the case of women, play can be similar to warming up an enginetoo much friction and heat early causes engine wear and tear. It is essential to take a gradual approach both physically and mentally.

Sexting can help you warm up, so that

you can be ready when we meet your partner.

The DO's and Don'ts of Sexing

There are no text messages between girls -This is the reason you have Girlfriends!

Sometimes, men act as soldiers from the films, who don't talk even when they are under threat of being tortured. Since they don't think talking about anything with something interesting, they feel uncomfortable. Discuss your day-to-day successes and other jovial things with your female friends. Your friends are, as they say girls, so the exchange of personal details that you share daily is normal and welcomed. Utilize your female friends as your source of information.

Eyes Are Desperate As well as in the Texts

They are able to detect fear, they talk about dogs. We speak of Dogs That Can Talk, you need to be aware of the fact that your fears can be evident in all your interactions. But you're not worried. You're the Woman with The Man Plan. Therefore, use sexts to convey positive, optimistic and sexual thoughts, not worried about whether the Ice cream you ate is leaking onto your hips (he hasn't noticed).

Beware of the more graphic "Art" Photos for Your Protection

We've all heard reports of the release of extremely private photographs of various stars, as well as politicians who have been found sending pictures from the "junk" for women who are not part of their marriages. Yes, a photo can convey the story of a thousand words. It is important to be cautious when posting pictures of ourselves because of two reasons. One, you don't like your male colleagues especially women from the older age group who might be able to observe you while in the suit. This is the same for family members and your friends. The photos could be embarrassing for them. Then, the vulnerability of electronic communications means that the photos you post could end getting distributed to more people than you are at ease with having such a thing as a cute mole in your ... It is our suggest that you stick to writing only. It's much more secure.

Don't joke about his man Parts. Offering encouragement is More Effective

We've discovered that the normal state

of men is competitive. They are competing with their male counterparts at work at sports, and even in obtaining women. They are all concerned about whether they will ... meet the standards with what they consider to be ... feminine gear. It isn't the meat; it's the manner in which a man goes about adhering to his duties as a lover. Therefore, give him the occasional "Atta Boy" about his most prized object; he'll be thankful for the praise and support.

Beware of Being Lost In Translation

Sexting is extremely hot, very sexy and extremely efficient. However, some words send the wrong message , and sound hot, not sexually attractive, and not efficient. We suggest that you stay away from more medical terms like vagina or penis. They are reserved for the doctor to utilize (and we're in no way talking about"the "Love doctor"). We recommend that you avoid locker room terms such as cunts and boobs to go with boxes and the tits. These sound sexier and less rough.

Chapter 2: Learn These Principles (Men Only)

Learn These Principles

#1 - She is not an individual and doesn't think like one.

Humans are extremely logical. We like to plan and make things clear using our minds and logic. Women, however, are highly emotional. You may think this is a complete generalization. However, it's actually the case of 80% or more of the time. It's the way females are. And only those with multiple masculine characteristics tend to be on the rational side. I'm sure that you could identify some instances that are based on your interactions with women. Even in the absence of any encounters with women, think about it by watching what you've seen on television as well as in Movies. There's a reason it is so common to hear guys...and girls tell you that "women are insane" since from a logic standpoint, they're almost. The girls themselves will say this!

Let me clarify what I mean by the form of a perfect example: "flaking'

Let's say that you and this girl have been rubbing the same notes. You are both enjoying yourself and connecting well. The two of you are having a fantastic evening filled with laughter and deep conversations.

You message her the following day to arrange for a date, and BAM. You get nada, zero, no response. If you're lucky, she could offer you excuses after every time you attempt to schedule a date.

You're probably considering... "Well how do I know ***, was I able to have done wrong? We had an amazing time"

Let me guide you into a situation so you are able to better understand:

Imagine this beautiful girl who was flaking on you. The day before, she was required to go to work an hour earlier. After returning home, she was able to realize she needs to complete her assignment for the Marketing 101 final. When you get home, send her a text right when she's on the 3rd page of her assignment.

The scenario you're probably thinking is "me texting her to make her smile!" What's actually happening It's that she's not in the same state of mind as she was on that night, and as a result (And because you've never had any training from the text) it's perfectly acceptable to be a jerk about the date, or even not send a text. Even if she's a fan of you! Another scenario you likely have seen is this. A group of women in the car listening to some good music on a sunny day, with the windows shut down. Have you ever been in a car such as this? They're smiling, having fun and wagging at everyone. It's like the music as well as the atmosphere has put her in an emotional state in which this feels natural and flows. Then, simply remove the music and people she has been with. Imagine that you could replay the entire scenario, but without these things. She won't be pointing at anyone. I can guarantee that. However awesome you may be. You can be a Channing Tatum lookalike wealthy, rich, and driving an elegant car, but she'll never have the confidence to make waves anymore, because she's not in the same emotional state.

There are some fundamental sets of strategies we'll learn in the future. She will see that you are a man with numerous women choices in his life as a man engaged in a successful life, and one who must make a conscious effort to keep. For now, remember principle #1 : she's not a man , and she is not thinking like one. Women are heavily dependent on their emotions.

#2 - You'll Only Falsify It Up To This Point

To get to the last point, when you engage in any kind of conversation, the aim is to let people view your character in a specific manner. If you're employed as receptionist at the front desk, you'll need to appear educated and professional. If you're speaking to a woman you'd like to look cool, or if you're going to an interview for a job, you need to look like an ideal fit. There's a great quantity we can modify to show her that she sees yourself as a mighty man. However, you're only able to fake it until you are sure.

You must be continuously making yourself better, and in doing this, you are embarking on a lifelong journey of improvement , you must think about it this way. What is the most disastrous outcome could occur? You will become a better person! It's true that there's no negative I can think of the pursuit of improvement in yourself.

If the girl you're interested is pretty attractive, guess what? You're not alone in messaging her! What is it that makes you different from the other guys between 4-10 who are texting her?

Here's the best way to tackle this. Start small and be proactive rather than reacting.

Make a start on improving something. Do you want to get into better condition? Get yourself into the gym. There is no need to be obsessed with being a model. Sure , it's a worthy ambition to aim for as a male, but women aren't as concerned about it as much as you believe. If you're well-groomed, women are much more concerned about the emotions you make them feel.

If you are in need of proof, I would suggest that you check out the photos to Instagram and Twitter. The models that women swoon on are just average-looking guys who have a more muscle, slightly more than average. These physiques require less than, or perhaps one year to attain.

The first step that a baby must master. Start doing the things to get more healthy, eat food that can make you feel healthy and content, begin wearing clothes that are stylish (no this doesn't necessarily mean expensive brands. However, clothing that fits your body well) even in the event that you don't know where to begin, just begin.

The second is being proactive rather than reactive. What I mean by that is... It was the case that I used to had fairly good teeth. It wasn't the most white of teeth, but no less than decent by any means. I bought an inexpensive whitening kit for $10 at Walmart and then did some research about the best brushes and toothpaste available and purchased them for just $10.

The transition from good teeth to a brilliant white set of teeth within 1 month and half. A different example is that my hands didn't look bad but I was suffering from calluses due to lifting, and the palms of my hands typically appeared dry. I did some research and discovered ways to remove the calluses with a Walmart grooming tool , called the primus stone. I also realized that I had dry hands as I was taking far too hot showers. In the end, I have smooth and clean hands. A final example that isn't physical is not something I've personally done, however you'll be able to understand the idea behind it. If you're looking to be more enjoyable, you can spend anywhere from 20 minutes to an hour every day watching comedy on YouTube in a matter of weeks that funny gene might begin to show up in your. The most important thing to remember from the second principle is to always work to improve your performance. Don't make up stories regarding your personal life. It's much simpler and more relaxing to live and lead a wonderful life, rather than pretending to be and dealing with all the small falsehoods that accompany it. Believe me when I say This is among the most crucial things. You'll be so content knowing that you're constantly striving to be better regardless of how little you're making progress and I'm almost able to assure you that it's been the case for me and

I've watched this happen to others who have committed to making changes each day by a tiny amount will completely surprise you in a year's time. Then you'll be reflecting on the year, wondering how much could be achievable in a single year. Each year you'll strive to improve the previous year and this is the way to an amazing life. Today, it's an instrument for teeth whitening, but next week it could be a new hairstyle next month it could be a brand new program for weightlifting and in four months it could be a side-business in a year's time you could be travelling more and little each day you'll get better and better. This is what top-quality people are composed of.

One year can change your entire life.

#3 - You must be messaging or texting several women and be a busy man

You're not in a relationship, so stop

trying to save yourself for that one girl. Most likely, you've seen Instagram tweets or posts about women who are looking for loyal men and not think about her and blah and blah. If you're in a formal non-open relationship, yes. If you're not talking with other women, and if you're not perceived by her as a man who has multiple female options in his life She will tell you to stop and be disqualified from a relationship based on your borderline. Really, it's that serious... Here's the reason...

One of the characteristics of a man which is loved by every woman admires is his sexiness... is, well, is a generalization to ALL women because of how significant it is (you are able to conduct your own investigation if you aren't convinced this) .... One of the traits that most women find attractive is a man who's working hard. This is the reason sportsmen and uniformed men are so attractive to women. They're men who are perceived to be doing something.

With the girls I go out with, I like to play games in which we boast about each one another. This is usually done after the second or so date . I would also suggest you give it a go. It's a constant exchange about the qualities you admire about one another. Every time, even girls who aren't sure about me, they always say the same thing "you have a clear idea of what you wish to get to achieve in life , and you're striving to get it". It's about communicating this message to her in a an approach that isn't direct.

If you tell someone "hey I'm wealthy" both genders are likely to think negatively of your character. If they find out by themselves that you're wealthy, they will think that they are more envious of them. It's the same person but how it was presented to them is what matters.

When you are busy doing some important work and texting other women often, and she'll see you as someone with something going on and is worth following.

This is a crucial aspect to know about guys. It is common for humans, female and male to want to be challenged, a pursuit of something. Consider this: why do you think the Aston Marin better than a Honda? Naturally, you'll be able to mention that it is better in terms of performance, quality, and appearance and that's all true. In the majority of human being, one of the greatest emotions is knowing that you possess something that isn't available to others. Rare = highly sought-after. This is the reason blue eyes are so appealing since they're a rare gene. The majority of people are brown-eyed. Making blue eyes rare.

You must be Aston Martin. The high-end, high-status man, a man who is hard to come by one who can read women and has a winning attitude to life. Imagine how wonderful you'll make her feel as this man, and letting her be aware that she has something not any woman could ever have. Do you know how powerful this will make her feel happy as opposed to a generic compliment.

This is the reason for the widespread belief that women are awed by assholes. There is no woman who likes to be treated as a shite (only few are suffering from serious health issues and require professional assistance). The asshole poses a big obstacle. He approaches every woman with the idea "this woman is beautiful, Let me check to see how she's doing to my standards". The woman is aware of his way of carrying himself, that he's an individual with a lot of women possibilities throughout his day. This is is extremely difficult to fake, and women will notice it when you try. You must live it. It's not about the asshole however, you must have standards and a mindset of abundance. Being aware that there are many women like her, and you can access them easily. Even with a sexy asshole having nothing or nothing to offer, women are drawn to them! This is a bit contradictory considering that the main point in #2 is about getting better at yourself and not pretending to be. However, I would like you to consider if an individual woman ever did the same thing to you. It was a test and gave you just enough time to make you feel comfortable, and made you feel as if you needed to prove yourself. It transformed you into the one who is desperate to chase her for a long time. It's seduction.

Both girls and guys are terrified of going back to "zero" after having spent the time and effort to build a relationship. However, nobody is willing to say'see you later and then move on. This is when the need for a break comes in.

Here's the key. We will transmit the message

We are busy performing important work

We text/talk to women

We have standards, and if she doesn't meet them, you can go on with it, without hesitation.

You are in charge but she'll end up following you. Through our words, talking and texting, we can create the impression that she must impress you and meet your expectations. It's true that THIS is what women want. So long as you're not swaying too much towards one direction. This allows you to use phrases such as "you're stunning whenever your smile", "you look incredible today" because the girl doesn't expect to be told that and since she's in the midst of following you, this helps her feel valued and makes her feel wonderful. You'll be able to appreciate those words more since you're not the normal nice guy who throws these around without even saying an appropriate hello!

Once you have an understanding of the attitude needed for women to be attractive, Let's move on to the heart of this book. Making use of your words to attract women, you must know.

Chapter 3: Attractions For Buildings

The days of one had to go through the hassle of actually walking up to someone to start a conversation. For men, it's difficult. imagine how difficult it can be for women just like you.

It is the action of engaging in a conversation with a flirt. The act of flirting is effortless when you are in face-to-face or in actual contact. Women like you are able to flip your hair with a seductive look, put on your smile with a sweet smile, and lick your lips, and men will be able to tell you're flirting. If you are doing it on via the telephone, you only have to do is alter your tone. Smile as you speak or chat sexually. However, flirting over an exchanging text message is an entirely different matter completely. You'll need more than just your hair and curves to begin creating a connection with your guy. What can you do to achieve this? Here's how:

In the beginning start by being the first one to introduce yourself. (See chapter 15 "Should I first text him"). You won't know if he's interested in you if you didn't attempt. Men also fear you already know. Make the first move so to say. The most crucial job of all. If you don't take this step, then nothing else will follow. Be sure to inform him that you are thinking of him. ("Hi how do you feel about you...i thought of you after I saw this film. ..."). Text him using his name. This will make the conversation more intimate and personal.

Second, you should use the colons, dots, or parenthesis when you use your smartphone (aka smiling). They're fun and flirty simultaneously. They'll definitely be overlooked. Body language plays a crucial part in communicating and smileys fill the gap left by body language when conversations are conducted via text messages. They help to clarify an intentions that words alone cannot convey.

:-) = happy

:-(= sad

;-) = flirtatious or sarcastic smiley

0 :-) = angelic smiley used after a sweet or innocent remark

> :-) = devilish smiley when a devilish comment is made

:-0 = shocked smiley that implies the sender is yelling or shocked with what is said

You can mix and match punctuation marks to make your smiley. For flirting you can send a hugs and kisses smiley that looks like this: []:*

Thirdly, you must learn to ask questions in the correct method. Although men may not be aware, but they love to talk about themselves just as women do. They discuss yourself. You should ask broad questions and open-ended questions rather than ones that can be answered with either a yes or yes or a. You will be able to become more acquainted with him by doing this.

Fourth, master the art of reading the text clues. You will be able to determine whether he has interest or not based on the speed of his response and response length. If he responded quickly or make longer messages and messages, then he's intrigued. If the response takes longer than normal or responds with one word, it's that it is time to take a cue and try again the next day.

Fifth , do your homework. The process of sending a message isn't so simple as telling someone how you are and hoping that it works from there. Engage in some healthy and acceptable boundaries cyber stalking. Discover his favorite sites. There's a chance that you're having a few things in common. Be careful when talking about the things you like and don't. Don't make it too obvious that you already knew the things he was fond of. If you do not agree over a couple of things don't be concerned. However, don't be apathetic about it. You can have a lively debate that is friendly and fun. It could become an inside joke when you are a target.

Sixth, men wanted be acknowledged in the same manner as women are. People were enthralled by compliments. Make sure you give your potential partner the praise that he deserves, or you lose the relationship. Don't compliment his looks right away. You might be thinking that he's just interested in looks, and not the entire package. Don't forget to include an image of a smile or two to the text message you send.

Seventh, make plans for future plans for the "future". If the conversation was flowing effortlessly, send suggestions of your future plans. Make a suggestion about plans to get together. A simple "let's meet for coffee sometime" can be enough to send an impression that you'd like to be spending more time together.

Chapter 4: What To Do Convert In The Man To Text (For Only Females)

Today, text messaging isn't just the most popular method of communication, it is widely used due to its practicality. It's a busy day ahead of you, and you've been asked to invite your friends to a celebration in just two days. Instead of putting your phone in your hand when you rushed between floors to accomplish the goals of the day then you create a similar text message, and then send it to the people you'll need, and you're done! Your party is ready. Texting is also a great way to serve as a teaser for conversations, at times where you want your spouse to give the issue some consideration before you discuss it in a one-on-one manner.

Short Messaging Service, either made up of cellular or internet-based networks, is commonly used during a relationship in the beginning to well beyond the point of crushing one another and into the relationship. But, gender differences in the way that text messages are sent, as mentioned in the past, can hinder the formation of solid relationships via texts. In our modern world there is a significant increase in women texting is greater than males. This is due to scientific research and women's unique way of expression and emotional connection to their phones as well as the people on their phones. Men however considers this to be an opportunity to communicate, that allows simple messages to be sent and received , and to the man's thoughts it is not required to respond. It's not always planned as people will tell you that, however, it is frequently performed, and that is where the problem in the relationship starts.

Men who are predators will spend the majority of their time searching for new targets and partners, while women live in their phones, ensuring constant communication with their loved ones. Texting is defined as a safe place for women who turn to their mobiles to escape certain situations , or simply put the world to sleep to get back to themselves. It doesn't matter if it's gossip, family interaction or even having a conversation with a partner or a spouse, it's all for emotional motives. However, the male is likely to pick up his phone, open the application for texting and establish new relationships with the other sexual partner with no passion. Because of the disconnect between the phone and the man women have almost the same complaint list in regards to receiving texts from a man , as well as receiving a reply to a message. The use of emoticons in poor quality, or even a lack of punctuation and, most importantly the absence of a response was on one of the most common errors made that men make when texting. However, it is now an ongoing battle between the genders since women have come to the conclusion that if a man doesn't reply within one hour it is likely that he won't return your calls and most certainly be late for the date. While men have denied this claim, being busy is not an sufficient explanation for the other gender.

There are significant differences between a man and a Woman when it comes to communication

Grooming
In the age of text messages women are

more likely to flirt with the man which is completely against traditional norms of society where men should groom his wife. In simple terms grooming is the act of developing a relationship with someone. It is the process of establishing a relationship, and create a sense of emotional connection and trust that draws the man in a subconscious way. This is sometimes referred to as manipulative, however today, the use of text messages have made women more powerful. A man's remark about a woman in a one-on-one conversation can be a challenge however, sitting in front of an electronic keyboard makes it much easy since embarrassment and shyness aren't visible. A man can perform very little grooming on text messages.

Questions
If you start conversations between two

partners you'll be able to see the female tendency to ask questions regarding various topics. This could range from "did you buy the bottles of wine from the store?" to "Did you take advantage of sex this evening?" These questions matter to women as they consider it as a method to convince the man to join to the table and create a stronger bond. On their other hand, view questions as the trigger for disputes and would do whatever to get around them.

Answers
Also, observing the conversation between spouses can give you an insight into what men typically do when having an exchange with the other sexual partner. They are the ones to answer questions asked by women. They're more likely to respond to a question without providing any explanation or

explanation. When texting, men respond to questions to avoid confrontation . They tend to withdraw from the conversation after providing answers.

Coordination

For males, the majority of conversations that are text-based whether it's between a man and woman, or men to men is governed by coordination. It's likely something you've heard before however, you'll soon be able to see that they are better coordination in their social lives, more so than conversators. Males are the same, and this improves communication and makes it more efficient since they work as machines.

Information

Men are great informants and you'll see that the information they provide is not the usual gossip or unnecessary banter. A man will send you a message about an upcoming event that should be given an attempt or about the most recent and most durable tire on the market and the best place to buy the tires. Women are, however will weave information and gossip. Most of the conversations will be focused on a particular topic, not only to get information.

Personal News
It is the most awkward thing for a male to tell a fellow male that his wife is three months pregnant. However it is common and expected for women to tell her friend she believes she's pregnant, even before conducting a pregnancy test. Women can share personal information in texts just as they would during one-on-one conversations.
In essence it is said that women are believed to function as an Central

Processing Unit (CPU) that uses technology to not only convey information but also create connections, build connections, and even cause the collision of two worlds. Men are often compared to the tools of logistical communication that work using one-word responses, or orders.

The differences in the way you categorize your messages on text in comparison to other sexes can help in getting your current or potential spouse in the process gradually but slowly but surely.

Turning Around Bad Texters
The worst of bad texting habits are a matter of ignoring Sometimes all your guy needs is a small education, but in a subtle way.

The Texter that is Passive-Aggressive

This is the type of person who gives only one word responses and expect you to know what they are trying to convey. After a long message you'll receive replies like "Okay," "that's fine," and this can result in a number of miscommunications and confusion. Someone who texts may need some kind of medication to allow them to see their mistakes. Although some people will remain blind to the reverse psychology, subtle reversal techniques will be a significant improvement to asking questions such as "what is okay?"

The Gusher
Many women have encountered someone who believes that all the universe revolves around him, and is actually texting like it. The kind of person will constantly text you about how much he dislikes his job, but will not quit

because one of his bosses is completely dependent on him. He worries about losing the health insurance. He will continue on and on about his life. In text messages you'll see that you just asked him what he's doing and then a lot of sentences about the life of his. In order to bring him back into life, don't have to embark to a texting frenzy with him since he's obviously talking to himself. You can give him the notorious digital space, pretending you didn't care and then he'll be able to see that all texts originate from himself. You could also dissuade him with a few worded responses or even inquire about his opinion about your hairstyle and it could be a reminder that there are other people all over the world.

The Shouter
The men are accused of using incorrect

punctuation while texting. one of them is the constant usage of capitalized letters. For instance, he may send you text messages like "GOOD AM, DID YOU sleep well?" first, ignore it , and then respond with a lower case. The texter is known to include exclamation marks without need and, to them, exclamations can make texting more exciting and not boring. If he continues to do this in this manner, it's time to play and play it in a funny way, or make him an emoticon that expresses dismay and ask him "Why is he shouting? Is everything okay?" he will realize the fact that he's using capital letters, and will activate the lower case button.

The Vowel Buyer

When we text, we are able to interact with a variety of characters. Buy-a-vowel is among the most popular. The person

who replies to your message with"K,"
"U," and a "K," "U," "l8r," all of which
mean okay, You, Later, or later. This isn't
just irritating and annoying, but also
frustrating. To bring him back to normal
it's necessary to inquire about what he is
referring to when he says "K." You is
likely to tire trying to explain every vowel
that he throws at you and then reset it to
default. Make it appear as if you are not
familiar with his insipid use of vowels,
and then get him to text in the words.

The Sexter
As the communication among you and
your spouse develops, sexting can be
permitted but in the appropriate
proportion. But, it is possible that you
are just beginning to get becoming
acquainted, and your possible spouse is
constantly sexting , and sending these
flirty messages, and even pictures. It's a

bit confusing because you're only beginning to get to know the person. On his part you could be doing it unknowingly because it's a habit it has built up over the years. Many men also conceal behind the sexting habit due to a lack of conversation or knowledge of how to express themselves. As a female you must keep him off the track without provoking or insulting him. Make sure you catch his attention and explain how uncomfortable it is to sext to you at this point. This might be a one-on-one conversation in which you watch his reactions and body language. This will allow you to determine if you are dealing with a genuine person or is just a normal person.

The Cliff-Hanger

Are you in an exchange with someone who left the conversation hanging and leaves you're not sure what they meant? The cliff hanger is that person who is unsure with his replies such as "If you'd like to" "Hope you've had a meal," or "I think I'll" in situations where you require an exact answer, not a hang-up one. In this case it is advisable to respond to the text with the phone, and politely ask what he is referring to. A couple of calls will allow him to get a taste of coffee and fix his poor behavior when texting. Tell him that you need an immediate answer to a question and then bring you to the center for a full discussion.

If you are trying to convince your guy or potential partner to texting issues however, do so with care. The first step is to recognize the differences in gender when texting and attempt to comprehend why he text the way you do. Texting isn't an issue of life or death, so don't take it too hard on your spouse.

Because it's an ongoing process of learning, you should reel him slowly and slowly and not bombard your partner with complaints left, right and all over the place. This can cause him to leave the relationship, or make him sway further into his cocoon. Additionally, in this phase it's fine to be flexible and meet halfway since you're probably not as flawless as you believe. You may also have some things to rectify with regards to your texting habits So, listening to him can assist in building a good relationship and a healthy communication in your marriage.

Chapter 5: The Things That Could Affect The Flow Of Your Discussion

The conversation you begin must be maintained so that she can feels your presence each when her mind drifts off of her busy schedule. This shouldn't be as if you're stalking, however, you must do it in a way that you are able to stay to her and she'll always expect for a response from you. Here are some suggestions for keeping an ongoing progression of your connection.

It is not enough time to keep the conversation going. Some people believe that waiting for a while when you're supposed to be talking to someone you've just discovered is an attractive thing to do however the truth is that you'll get annoyed with the woman by making her believe that you were bored with the way you communicate.

If you've had an easy conversation with your new woman, she'll be keen to continue the conversation because an exciting relationship can be thrilling for women. They would like to push it to the very highest possible level which is why if you don't communicate, she could feel demotivated and be lost as soon as you have her.

The right reaction for delayed responses Girls can be in a mean way at times by delay in replying, to give you the need to reach them. Sending messages to them due delay in replying gives them an adrenaline rush as it's a way to let them feel loved, appreciated and unique. But, don't interpret the strategy in a way that suggests that she's bored with you, or perhaps she is bored.

Give it some time and stay clear of all negative reasons you might be contemplating. The ex hasn't been seen

since, and she's not losing interest in you
, and it's not because she's not willing to
welcome you in on her journey. Stay
away from these negativity thoughts,
and allow nature to follow its course.
Doing your best to think about the delays
in replies will just add stress to your
shoulders for no reason.

Some girls get hard and choose not to
respond to messages or even cancel
plans you had planned like going out for
a meal together. If this happens, try to
keep your cool and forget the fact that
you feel bad about the situation, but
deep in our hearts we know that you'll
be suffering terribly and you should wait
until the moment she'll reply.

The wait should not be long, but allow
her a few days before reaching out to her
once more. If she just played rough,
she'll show up and offer an apology, but
also give an excuse, too. Sometimes

people don't want to look like they're chasing you. However, a woman may be the same way again, and as a man, you need to prove your worth, and let go. Don't try to contact her as if she's interested , she will respond to you. The key is to not quit when you encounter an emotional reaction from a new beautiful woman. Give it some time until she gets settled and is convinced that you truly desire her.

You may be wondering why she's so in a way that isn't logical? Making women attract her to you isn't an easy task. You must realize that it is a matter of patience, work and perseverance, as well as humility. The emotions of women are extremely fragile, and you should accept her for what she is since you're both strangers to one another, and she will need time to get to know you before she can either accept or deny your proposal.

With that said it is important to remember that everyone is different, and, while some may be willing to accept your offer while others may take days to get into the groove. One of the advantages of being in a position where you're communicating is that the majority of women aren't going to be able harm your feelings by refusing to accept you. They are not a fan of dramas that pop out of confrontations, because they end up being ugly.

The desire to do well throughout the day causes them to take a take a step back and let nature to run its course which can lead to the where you are ready to give up or trying to get more attention. If you are negative to a woman's reaction, she will justify her feelings and conclude that she is not the type for you However, if you show an interest that is greater and carry on to pushing with enthusiasm, you'll eventually win her over.

Some girls may not be a fan initially but based on how they're wired, she will not be able to be rude or show any feelings towards you. This is the reason you'll notice the lack of understanding that they display. It will not last in the event that you realize that she wasn't just waiting to be wooed by you to be her perfect man It is your responsibility to sow the seed of attraction to you in order for her to give you the attention that you would like, and respond to your texts quickly.

The best things don't come quickly, so you need to put in the effort to find the gorgeous woman you meet. There will be an "No" in the course of your journey and probably a few to be exact. You shouldn't feel hurt or disappointed by the first rejection. Genuine women will make sure that you really want to stay with them, not playing about.

The idea of slapping a girl for having rejected you for a while isn't the right way to handle the problem. Some men accomplish great things and buy expensive gifts in order to win acceptance only to end up empty with nothing. However, your efforts should be measured in order to identify the level of resistance, as you can surely be able to identify genuine resistance when you are likely to achieve an advantage.

Let a girl tell you about the feelings she feels about you, and make sure they are real. Saying that she doesn't like you isn't an end in itself since you are able to come up an answer to the reason that is making her feel that she doesn't like you. Find out more from her as often as you can. However, avoid being too aggressive as she might not respond to or even ignore the messages she receives from you.

Be sure to text her only in the event that she is willing to respond and if she becomes dull, you can slow down a bit or even ask whether she would like to talk to you to discover what you can do to end the impasse.

Be sure to keep your texting calm and under control as there are women who does not respond to "yelling" messages very kindly and could turn out to be the final word. Begin the process of looking for an attractive woman knowing you have two faces of the coin. You may be rejected, or accepted, however each process takes time. Ladies allow time for the initial conversation to get to know their potential suitors, and the result of their evaluation will determine whether they either reject your approach or give you a thumbs-up and you'll be able to take another step in the process of getting a spot in the heart of the gorgeous lady.

What is the reason that the numbers you are given don't work Do you have any idea what makes every single number you request from women you meet do not lead to a real relationship? Be calm because you're not alone and this is a reality for numerous men across the globe. We have a solution this guide, and the best part is that you do not have to think about within your capabilities to find a solution for this. The issue is what you do with the number you've been given. When you are approached by a woman who is willing to give you her number, the ball is in your hands. Your expertise and your determination to pursue the woman can help you beat her.

In this scenario the girl's role is to only give you her phone number and you're required to take all actions related to relationships, including reaching to her beauty. That is you have to start the conversation and push the conversation forward. If the conversation becomes stagnant just accept that you haven't done your best. If you really want to meet the woman to take you seriously, you need to make it a point to push harder. There's always a chance even if the lady hasn't turned you off in a formal way and if she isn't keen on your decision, she will do all she can to put you off. This might not be a direct stop, but every time you'll try to talk to her, she'll go insisting that you're in the wrong direction and you need to look at a alternative.

Let's revisit the issues you face in making having a number come to fruition. We have previously stated that the primary reason to text the woman you've seen and enjoyed is to get her attracted to you and arrange for a date. you'll pour your heart out and let her know that you are never too late when you think about her. It is by the way you write your messages. The first ones you send should be beautiful and intriguing. Texts that inspire her to read them over and over again when you are at home.

Begin with fun and engaging texts that hint at your attraction to her and also the things that attracted the you towards her. The advantage of these first text messages is that you'll get a clearer idea of her responses and that is what will provide you with material for your next responses. When the texting is progressing you can take the next step "Hey By the way, we could have a drink on Saturday. Can you schedule an appointment for it?" Such requests however should be made after you have read her previous responses that demonstrate she's already comfortable and is willing to be a part of your team. The majority of men are hesitant to ask about whether she will be ready for the date, but this worry isn't justified as the majority of women are waiting for these moves as they cannot make the decision. You might encounter a small amount in resistance but this kind of resistance is one that has some solution or doesn't have as significant weight that it makes your request not come through. For example, she might say to her... "I might not be available as I am cleaning my laundry in the early morning time." She provides you with the hint that she may have come if not because of the laundry she's going to be doing in the morning. But then you'll push her insisting that she be available during the late evening which actually is the best time to get coffee at the end of the day's work. She may accept it, but in her heart she knows she has to get in touch with you.

Invite her for dinner or a cup coffee at a nice gathering spot, where you can unwind and have a more meaningful conversation one-on-one. The ideal time to invite the woman to come to your place isn't yet, and therefore avoid messaging anything regarding having a great time together at your home. The conversation about your house is best done after you've been used to each other or when she asks questions about your home. It is always suggested that you do this in the first moments of communicating and becoming acquainted with one another.

When you receive a rejection from your first request to a date, do not stop sending her messages. This could cause her to feel like she was wronged Perhaps all you want to do is meet her as quickly possible. If you're planning to invite her to the evening, you shouldn't be a sly naive about the matter. This will portray you as a snob who isn't sure what he really wants. Send her a text and be clear that you would like to having coffee, dinner or lunch on her time. In this moment it is important to base everything on the comfort of the girl. She is unique and you would like her to be satisfied with you. There is no way to impose your preferences on her.

If you inquire about the date in a casual manner You will be able to find out if she's really interested in you and then you'll leave instead of being a slave to the person who doesn't even consider you.

However If she does accept your invitation, you shouldn't end the opportunity to convert. Sending her texts regularly lets her know that you're still thinking about her, and the offer isn't over. The regular texting indicates that the enthusiasm you showed when you first started sending messages, or even when you convinced her to giving you her contact number is alive and well. Being able to text her until she is ready to set the date is a huge accomplishment. It is therefore important to ensure that you keep the achievement going by sending greetings throughout the morning, or if you do not get there, you should inquire about her day at night.

The goal is to make her aware to ensure that the date is in your thoughts. There are even stories in which you explain how you got there in the cafe you're planning to visit and then sipped a cup the beverage, then remind that you are aware that it would have been more enjoyable if she had been there.

The confirmation of the date can be made by texting her on the day prior to the date. You'd like to know whether the contract is in place and it's not appropriate to inquire to do this directly, by texting her on the day prior to the date will receive a precise answer of her position on it. The beginning of the fantastic day is the perfect moment to see how issues are. You can do this by texting and telling her how thrilled you are and how you hope to have the time of your life speed up to meet her in the near future.

Her reply to your texts will inform you if the two and you're on the same page or if she decided to alter the date. It's very heartbreaking to find out in the last minute that the date will not be happening. Be sure to confirm it prior to heading out to get her will ease your anxiety as well as your feelings. Although you'll be hurt and a bit broken but the impact won't be as severe as if you discover the news in the last second.

Limit your texting when you decide on the time of your meeting. But, if the messages come from her side, you should not ignore them. Answer her texts like you would normally. You are the one who needs her company so the texts is not to be ignored. In actuality, you're the one responsible to slow things down firstly to ensure that you do not ruin the excitement and, secondly, to keep some of the important and fascinating topics that you will need to discuss to discuss when you finally meet.You should have ample sources of material and topics to be able to utilize on the time of your date. It is not a good idea to be glued to each otheror replying to her chat's brief questions.

Engaging the reader as it develops

The act of texting a girl could be a quick or long-term affair, based on the way you handle it. There are some men who can't keep a girl interested in a texting without not having something to say to your new friend at some point, and they both become bored and stop the conversation. Today, where all communication is conducted by texting across various platforms like Whatsapp, Facebook messaging, Imo, Viber and many others, it is necessary to collect a wealth of information about various subjects to keep conversations going. One method is to discover what interests the new person you've discovered and then build your conversations around the various areas of interest. You could also present the things you enjoy to her in order that, at some point you can discuss the things you like, and she'll accept the things you like and join in.

But, you must realize that if you prolong your texting excessively long and at regular intervals, it is likely that you will be the one who loses. In fact, if you are spending too much time messaging the beautiful new girl it reduces the likelihood of seeing her in person since you'll end up discussing the various aspects that inspire you to see her. There is no doubt that you want something to happen , but getting this can be a challenge when you don't have a method to make the woman want to be around you. The best way to make the woman feel special is to be less talkative but make sure she is engaged enough in the knowledge that you are ever thinking of her. Additionally you must also realize that the impact of a conversation in person can't be compared to the impact of the conversation you are having when you text. The facial expressions and gestures you use have special abilities to make girls feel appreciated and will desire you to talk to them, even through your eyes.

The reason you should use the specific phrases you choose to use when texting is to attract your girl's attention which is why you must work that she will respond positively to an invitation to the date. Make it fun, but don't overdo it as it could degrade the quality. Couples who are happy have not met solely through texting however, the strength of the first part of their connection was achieved via text messages so that they would become familiar with one another.

Chapter 6: Writing The Type Of Texts That Bring You To The Top Of Your Mind And In The Heart Of His

Happy, flirty and positive texts are fun to read and make people feel positive and happy when they receive them. Clingy, sad or desperate looking texts aren't enjoyable for anyone. They can cause someone to feel depressed or even fearful. Everyone doesn't want to think they're dating a possible stalker.

Therefore, keep your flirtexting messages brief and sweet, fun and enjoyable or spicy and strong and you'll be just fine. If you feel you're coming across as clingy, pause and think about whether you'd consider someone to be stalker to send you the exact message.

If yes, then don't send that message.

Hey, I'd like to meet you on Saturday. What is the date? and other flirting questions?

Are you able to ask someone to go out for dates via text message? If you are just starting out, it could be a bad idea unless you've already established a pretty constant texting relationship. Some people aren't large phone users and prefer text messaging to keep in touch.

Some people are not so, and you need to be familiar with the person you're seeking out. This is a warning: if you don't know them enough to know what their preferred method of communication is, and how they communicate, then you are not knowing them enough to invite to go out on dates!

Other questions you could ask while flirtexting:

* What's your outfit Hot stuff?

* Are you thinking of me as I'm thinking of you.

* When do I get to kiss you again?

Texting and Etiquette

It is possible to ask whether texting someone after a date is acceptable and, if it is then who should you text. It's perfectly fine to message someone you've just had a date with, particularly in the event that they've stated that they are fond of calling or texting but not phone calls.

A short, "hey, that was enjoyable, thank you!" text is great and straight to the point. If you are the one who paid for the date Give your date the chance to send this message to you.

If he doesn't respond within the next day, you may send a brief, "I had a nice time" and sit and wait for a response.

If, however, your man paid , then absolutely send him a thank-you message whenever you feel it's appropriate. If you divide things equally, it doesn't matter who first texts.

You can break a date but You're Not able to Break Up with a text

Sometimes, circumstances arise and you need to cancel the date. If you're in no rush to make a decision until the last minute, you are able to send a text. If you're in an emergency, you can call him for a short call to clarify what's happening and apologize.

If he is unable to answer, then, leave a thorough message to his voicemail, and hope you get it before leaving to pick you up or take you to the agreed place.

You can request to alter the location, time or even who picks up who. You can do any of this, but you are not able to break up with someone by text message, for example.

If you've been with someone for long enough that you consider it as a "break up" then you must give him an open conversation, heart to heart regarding the reasons things aren't being well and what you can do to make them stop.

However it is possible that you've had a date or two but have never actually become the couple you are or even a couple, then you're in no way breaking off with your partner. You may certainly decline your dates by text, and if they don't take it seriously after a few rejections, you can state that you aren't keen on continuing to go any further.

Send, Wait. Resend. Wait A Little More. What Should I Do Now?

You sent your girlfriend a text message, but received no response. You are now contemplating whether you should send the text or if you need to do something else.

Be aware that you should not duplicate an email! There's nothing more frustrating than opening your phone and finding five identical messages that are evenly spaced over 10 minute intervals.

Send a message that is from your heart, and then goes to the heart of your loved one. If no response is received within a reasonable amount of time, then you can send another message and sit.

If, after an acceptable amount of time, you do not receive a response, then simply walk away and let him get back to you. He could be driving, or busy or in a location that doesn't have phone service. Do not make assumptions about the situation and don't play the character of a jealous oddo.

Here's a little bit concerning this issue that you need to be wary of: if your crush has not been in contact all day and hasn't responded to one text, but has sent you a message at night, this could be an issue.

There must be a legitimate reason for why he hasn't sent a single text and the late-night text is simply a disrespectful gesture of total disrespect. I'm not sure how to put it, but you've been locked in the booty call land.

If you let this persist, then he'll continue to annoy you. If he is able to provide an reason such as school or work obligations, there could be an argument but even the busiest of busy people will get a few minutes throughout the day to message someone they'd like to speak to if they truly want to connect with them, they'll make the suitable time.

Chapter 7: I Shouldn't Have Sent That!

It's all too common You send it and then you immediately regret you did it. If it's an obscene late-night booty text simply because you're lonely or if it's an innocent joke that was taken way too far, or a message you are certain is likely to be misinterpreted and the recipient will forever look at you in the same way. Of course, there's always the "Oh I didn't intend to write your friend," or "Haha, I'm just kidding," followed by a bunch of emoticons. There's nothing more frustrating than the feeling that builds in your stomach when the message bubble is blue and you can see "viewed as "time date" and then no response. Be assured that your burgeoning relationship isn't dead. Therefore, you don't have to rush to sign up on Match.com and change your status on Facebook to "Its

Complex," just relax, you'll be able to salvage the conversation and your relationship. Give it some time. Don't be too difficult on yourself We've all been there. it. Don't believe that you're at the bottom of the road since it's not. You're likely to think that what you wrote is more damaging than what he sent. In order to avoid sending those messages be a problem, keep in mind that you don't need to respond immediately. In some cases, you are so enshrined in their brain cells that you must respond as quickly as you can. Be patient, sketch some ideas then think about the possibilities and then act. I know this sounds silly to you can open an Word Document on your computer and write in a few possibilities to see what you like most appealing. Once you've got the rhythm down , you won't need to spend a lot of time thinking of the perfect return phrase. There's a misconception that if someone doesn't respond to messages within a specific period of time, it means that there is something wrong, but it's not. In other words, if they don't reply for three weeks it could be that they've left and if they've not returned a text within a couple of hours, it could be that they're at work or maybe eating lunch with their grandma or maybe they're just in the middle of their day. Don't fret. Make time to think over how this conversation might take place and the best way to guide it to the next level. Be sure to be always one step ahead and being focused on the end purpose that is to create an even deeper bond and connection. If you're a constant drunk, make sure you give your phone to your female friends before you go out to the bar. Guys don't like anything more than the a.m. "Hey! What are you doing?" Especially when they respondthinking that they might be invited over to be lucky, and you respond with "I Juest want to skjteaj tejakejr!" It's not cute and is no more offensive than the standard "Sorry for the messages you sent the other night," message at the beginning of the day. It's best to call a spade a spade, both of you already know that you're drunk We've had it all before, there's it's not necessary to apologize and if you really sorry, you wouldn't allowed it to take place. The best way to deal with that scenario is to do you know,) not drink too much or to) make your girlfriend place the mobile in the purse to ensure that you don't have to send messages to everyone on your contact list . Or c) make your favorite drunk text's number on an oversized piece of paper and place it in your desk drawer then remove his contact number from your phone in order that, when you leave to dinner, you will carry your phone and you'll be physically unable to text the message that you're embarrassed to send.

We've all sent messages we regret and often times we believe that they're worse than they really are. Do not be concerned, there is still a way to make improvements and save the relationship. Next chapter, you will learn to perform damage control. In the following chapter, you will also discover when it's appropriate to end the relationship, in the event that there's been too many terrible texts exchanged back and forth which is due to "oh you're right I shouldn't have done this," or a "we really have nothing in the same." Below, you'll notice the difference between what I actually mean by.

Chapter 8: What Does He Mean By That Text?

One of the difficulties when texting is that it's difficult to detect a subtle tone or end the sarcastic message by a laugh. This means that things can be misinterpreted. If you're unsure about something , you may inquire. However, in the majority of situations, unless you need to be aware of simply relax. It's easy to figure out what he was saying through his other writings.

If he's responding with simple one-word texts, then it's likely that he's busy or not in the mood to send a text in the moment.

Don't believe that he isn't eager to chat with you simply because he's not sending one message after the other. Also, he could be working. Don't dismiss him since he's probably not messaging you. What happens if he is constantly breaking dates with text?

If it happens at all, it's not likely to be a big issue. It could be that he is sick and he could be in the middle of work or school assignments or even his parents might decide to go out with the family the night before.

Do not respond with a sour, "You're such a jerk." You must be a good friend to him.

He could really be sick, or perhaps he's one of those people who don't have a good plan. Also your parent might have informed him that last month that the entire family would be celebrating grandma's 90th birthday , which falls on the 22nd of the month and he did not add it to his calendar. In this instance it is your responsibility to let him go but you must you can expect him to be better next time.

If you've had a second last minute

change of plans , you have to think about whether the person is trying to avoid the date. If he decides to cancel at least three times it's his own story. Of course, I'm not talking about that third cancellation in the space of two years, but rather three times at the beginning phases of dating him.

Chapter 9: Tips To Flirt With Texts

How can you tell him your interest in him is through texting?
Be playful. Do not take texting as serious initially. Relax and let the conversation happen or not. If you begin to stress about the "does the guy is like him?" or "will he ever want to ask me out?" then your texts are likely to become a bit sexy. Concentrate on having fun.
Do not respond immediately. Make it difficult by letting him sit and wait for

your response. Don't be apathetic about his messages throughout a period of stretch. However, be careful with your responses.

Find your own way to be creative. Don't be a victim of the old "Try to appear like dumb blonde" phrase. It's fine to let your friend know you're clever and clever and skilled at quick responses. It's not the time to discuss science or the fall and rise of the Roman Empire however you can show him that you're at a similar level to him. In order for a relationship to be able to endure tension, there must be harmony.

Should you approach him? Most likely not. Does he think less of you if we ask to speak with him first? It's unlikely. But you did break the tension. Let him discover ways to get you to go on an evening date.

You can drop a few hints. "Have been to

the latest Batman film, already?" This type of hint is more effective when you're not asking about the most recent chick flick. Chances are that you haven't seen the latest movie for chicks, or unless he took another girl to the theater.

Innuendo can be used to text when it's not too much.

Let me clarify: flirting is a game. It's not a requirement to play the game, or an liar, or clown. But the act of flirting can be compared to an ancient game.

If you're in a relationship and you've been out a few times , the dynamics alter. However, when trying to draw attention to someone else, you have to be creative and not predictable.

It's not a good way to meet one the other. It's best to wait until when you're chatting in person, or even using the phone.

Chapter 10: 7 Things You Should Learn

Texting can be a fantastic method of getting a man attracted to you, provided you do it in the right method.

Texting can make you appear desperate If you're not cautious. Beware of this at all cost.

Texting is a great method to look funny and smart. Think about what you'd like to communicate.

Texting is a great method for him to know you're not the only person on the planet. You're not waiting for him you.

The sarcasm in texts can be a deterrent. Most often, sarcasm is effective because the person you're talking to is able to discern what you're saying, how your voice sounds, way you roll your eyes, as well as many other indicators that suggest that your words are not what you're saying. With text messages, all these cues aren't available. You "think" about them in your mind. However, all he can see are the words you compose. Therefore, make sure that you're talking about something that could be taken as literal when you're actually just playing. Of course, you can always continue with the standard "lol and"j/k!" but this has become somewhat repetitive and sometimes even absurd.

Emoticons are a great way to express yourself - but in small doses. One text per day or two is sufficient. If you're using more than three emoticons per text, then you're probably addicted and have to quit. Also, try not to be a maniac with the emoticons you employ. For example, some users have attempted to express their extreme happiness by switching between "XD" or "XDDDDDDDDDDD" that really isn't a good idea.

It's not smart to text while driving. Let

the driver stay quiet until you've reached your destination. So, you won't seem desperate, and you won't hurt yourself, your family members who are traveling along with you or a complete stranger.

Chapter 11: Flirty And Sassy Texting Strategies

Text messaging flirting is among the quickest and easiest ways to get a guy's attention and keep him interested long enough to want to meet you on the date of his life-time.

When you're flirting with him through text messages, you must be able to balance being both evocative and sly. You should initiate but then let it go to let him assume the lead and feel confident This, in turn, plays into his instinctual desire to feel like the other person is following him and winning your heart.

To achieve this, use the below texting strategies for:

8 flirty and sassy texting Strategies to make him hot for you

These flirty and flirty messaging

strategies will keep you in his thoughts throughout the day and his love for you exploding like magma gushing out of the active volcanic eruption. Make use of them with care.

#1 Send him explicit text messages

No matter if you're a sultry romantic or a fierce vixen who isn't afraid to express her sexual desires and send flirty, sassy and sexually explicit texts will attract him to you.

Inspiring and sexually explicit texts can get him so gorgeous that he'll desire to invite you to dates just so that you can sit with you. He could also increase your chances of getting you to sleep since, surely, this not what you're looking for? You are able to be as direct or as subtle as you'd like and based on the kind of relationship that exists between you and the man you're talking to. For instance, if have been on a couple of dates with him and he been kissing you, you may send him a flirty or sassy late-night text message that reads, "Thinking about your kiss makes me swoon," or "Guess what I'm in the mood for right this moment?" When he replies to your question, you can add, "A deeper, prolonged version of the kiss."

Being honest and then taking a step back to let him run the reigns will keep you in his thoughts all day.

#2: Don't say you what to do, but imply

Man's imagination can be a powerful tool you can employ against him to keep his attention in his thoughts and create his desire for you.

For him to be unsure as to what you're thinking, doing, or even what you are saying keep a balance between being honest (step 17 and 18)and being more implicative. At times, stimulate your imagination, interest and interest by sending him messages that are implicative as opposed to direct ones. For instance for messages like "I cannot stop thinking about you" ...,"", or "when I have your attention" ..." will start getting the imagination of your recipient going. Without any doubt, he'll immediately begin to think about the various things you're thinking about or about what you'll do once you meet him.

Consider this method as a teaser. It's like showing a little your cleavage, leaving the rest to imagination. The subtleness of these message will help keep your in the edge of his thoughts.

#3: Laughter will take you a long way

Texting him funny messages will not only keep him in mind It will also make you look super hot, to the point that after engaging his funny bone He will want to take the relationship to the next level, turning it into a romantic date that can lead to more -- whatever you'd like actually.

Sending him a text message that makes him smile will immediately show him that, despite being an extremely driven woman, you're amusing, welcoming and open to lighthearted conversation. This will likely pique the interest of him and inspire him to learn more.

If he is a fan of jokes and jokes, then send him jokes. If you share a love of humorous memes and sarcastic jokes and memes, then send him some at the right moment of course. This will enhance the bond between you.

#4: Lead the way -- sometimes

While men like to be in control and he's eager to chase youaround, you're an independent woman which means that every once in a while you must display your determination by controlling the conversation and steering it to the direction you wish it to be headed.

Text flirting is an excellent chance to take control of the conversation which you can utilize to steer the conversation towards whatever you'd like, perhaps you'll be able to arrange a date in the near or in the near future.

For instance If you think you're handsome and want the guy to understand that you consider him attractive, being explicit about it is fine but only if, immediately after cooling off, you allow him the chance to be the one to lead and build a relationship. You could send him a text message similar to, "I think you are very attractive."

#5: Stay mysterious

Texting him can stimulate to his imagination and prompt naughty responses. If he does respond you, you are allowed to be unpredictably in your replies and keep your reader in suspense.

Consider an instance where you send a flirty or flirty message, which says you're naked because you skipped laundry day this week. Because you've sparked his interest enough to cause him to ask you if you're naked, make use of smiley or wink emoticons and alter the subject. This will awaken his curiosity and desire for you.

#6 The casual naughtiness

For flirting with him via text messages and thus keep him interested, use simple naughty texting techniques. For example, look for methods to make him consider your physique, or even that you're thinking about him.

You could casually talk about how you're about to enter the shower or left the shower and you are across the floor -- or how wonderful it is to snuggle under blankets in cold weather. In the end, a little imagination can never go wrong.

#7 Make him see something

Sexting isn't for everyone , and unless the individual in question is someone you've decided to stay with for the long haul then you shouldn't be sending him naked.

But even if you aren't able to sext him doesn't mean that you can't give him something sexually attractive to consider; as it is your creativity and have a good imagination, you can come up with visually appealing messages. For instance, if , for example, you purchased a brand new lipstick color and you want to make him send a sexually sexy picture of your lips, with the text "Does this lipstick shade make my lips smoky enough to take a bite of?" If you just bought a dress that exposes your cleavages, you can send him a sexy picture with the text "I'm pretty glam but I don't have anyone to go out with a pouting or sad emoticons."

#8: Maintain fluidity

It is crucial to be aware that texting is extremely similar to conversations in person; in both cases, you're sharing opinions and ideas, you're communicating. It is crucial to be fluid, unpredictably and in the right direction. If you follow the suggestions in this article this guide, you will create attraction. And since you have ignited his curiosity, imagination and desire to be with you The texting will turn to a potential date.

Secret Sexting Strategies That Work , Revealed

You don't need to be an expert on rocket

science to comprehend what sexting actually is. If you've lived under the rock of the cave Sexting is the digital equivalent of foreplay or pre-foreplay.

Like foreplay, sexting certainly not something every person is naturally skilled at. ("Amen" I've heard the female readers affirm).

If you're not careful, you may end up with an over-exaggerated idea of your sexual abilities which could result in a great deal of disappointment when it is right be able to prove your worth (pun is not meant to be intended). And, even more troubling, you may find naked photos of yourself online!

Before you dive into the techniques that go into sexting, there's some things to consider. Cyberspace is a risky environment, and you must ensure that you are protected as much as you can. There are three basic guidelines to follow when you are scrubbing your fingers.

Rule No. 1:
Never, ever reveal your face. Ever. If you decide to post photos of yourself in a birthday dress to the online world, who will decide? But you must always conceal your identity in order to be prepared for worst-case scenarios. This being said it is also important to not send naked photos of yourself to anyone you don't trust completely. It is also recommended to immediately erase any pictures that aren't yours off your phone once you've received or shared them, to shield each other from being humiliated.

Rule number two:
Before sending a message, think to

yourself if the message you're texting about is something you would talk to that person in real life.

Recite it and see whether it is appropriate to speak it. It is difficult to know what is acceptable to speak about and what's not unless you're acquainted with the other person very well. This leads us to the following rule:

Rule Three

Make sure to do the act at least twice before you sext. If you've not had a sexual encounter with the person at most several times, you aren't aware of what they're up to sexually, or what their boundaries are. There's a high possibility that you will be able to scare them away. Certain people require patience to adapt to new ideas , and If you're patient, this could result in very exciting times for your sext relationship.

Strategize, Strategize, Strategize

Like many other activities that we undertake, the success relies heavily on having a solid strategy or game plan, an approach to determine the best approach to take for the greatest benefit. Sexting can be a success and, if it is done correctly it can result in an extremely enjoyable and intimate experience.

* Text before you send a sext. To avoid tragedy, make sure that your partner is attentively looking over your text message and watching your phone's secure setting prior to sending anything that is too explicit. This can be accomplished by sending brief messages that are not sexual during the course of your day. If your companion receives your message only within a couple of

hours of having sent it, your moment may be gone, and could be an offender. It is important to understand his or her timetable and figure out the most suitable time to start flirting.

Keep the audience with a smidgen of doubt. Avoid giving away too many. This will increase anticipation and , in turn, excitement. Make sure to say only what is important to set your partner's imagination to run wild. If you're a woman you can try such a thing as "I am betting you won't identify the color of my pants that I'm wearing" or for an individual, you could say: "You are in for something unique tonight. I'm sure you're ready". Don't forget to include an emoticon that blinks can add an extra spice to your message.

* More is less. Many people get caught up in their sexts and then end up

overdoing it with their Sexts. They notice that it initially works well and then get into doing it every day. Why fix something that's broken, isn't it?

Similar to the strategy that keeps them guessing the more you can tell, using sexting in a moderate manner will keep it exciting and efficient. Additionally it will entice and enthralle your partner more when he isn't sure when to expect another sexy text message.

* Don't let yourself be bored. If you're bored, it's entirely your fault. Why? While the sexting process have a lot of similarities with real sexual sex, physical contact is clearly missing. To compensate the gap, it's essential to be creative and communicate with your partner what's or isn't working for your. Your partner should take the same action to ensure

that you're at the same level and understand what you can do to make your sexting enjoyable and interesting. To begin, one method to accomplish this would be to create cute names for sexting for each other. Names for pets which are solely used for sexting.

It doesn't matter if you're trying it to enhance your marriage or simply to enjoy a night out with your spouse it is in the air. It can be an efficient tool, but it could also cause harm.

Always be active and be aware before hitting the button to send!

Most importantly, make sure that you plan ahead and make certain that both you and your co-worker remain on the same level.

Chapter 12: When Does Texting Become

Texting can be a great method of communicating with others, especially family members, but like everything else there are limitations to it.

If you're texting someone you just met recently, it is not advisable to give out too much of your personal details about you. You should take a variety of factors into consideration before sharing intimate details about your private life, as it could affect your reputation, or even your relationship. It is better to do it slowly but definitely.

It can be a means of capturing the imagination of a person through sexual approaches. It may be a less level of seduction however is there a safer method of flirting? Yes it is. Making fun of her or complimenting her on her appearance and how attractive she looks are considered better alternatives.

It is not advisable to ask too many questions, as it may appear like you're asking her questions or appear too desperate.

The idea of bombarding her with a plethora of messages is not a good idea. Nobody wants to read and delete a lot of irrelevant messages. Sending a few messages could help her keep her texts and keep them for a long time. Text bombing could cause you to appear at her in a desperate search for a response. It is a good idea that you wait until she has a response prior to sending another text message. In this way the conversation will flow without a hitch and won't become complicated. It can be frustrating to receive text messages throughout the day long from the same individual. This can make you appear like someone who is stalking you.

It is also important to keep in mind to

only flirt in situations that are mutually comfortable for both of you. It is a period where you've already laid the basics for an upcoming relationship. Women respond to flirty comments differently. Certain girls might consider them harmless while other might consider you to be an obnoxious pervert. It is important to be careful about what you say before you send any message to ensure that you don't damage the things you've put into.

You should be so interested about someone, but you shouldn't be letting her know that you are interested. Women can play at getting you to recognize that you're attracted to them. Do not send text messages that resemble novels. While it might provide a better understanding of what you're talking about, it may be boring for her. Avoid asking "Watcha doin'?" at least once in a while. Be sure to not ask her what she had for lunch, breakfast or dinner. Even her mother doesn't inquire about her activities during the day. This can make you appear too intimate.

It is best not to bother her when she states that she's busy. Space is a key element in any relationship. It provides a person with time to accomplish the tasks they need to take care of for themselves or. Also, giving space means respecting the time of the other to do other things important.

Be understanding of your feelings. Do not force her to reveal why she's sad , even though she doesn't want to. Do not force her to send a contact you when she's not feeling well. Being able to tell someone that you understand her can be a great comfort and can bring great rewards. She will open up about her feelings when she is sure it's the right moment and is more comfortable with you.

If she replies "Bye," do not transmit a second text. This indicates that she's done with the conversation , or is doing something else. You should not send her a text until she texts you back.

Be cautious when using acronyms too frequently. A complete sentence is easier to be read. The correct spelling and grammar is crucial because it gives the impression that you're an educated and sophisticated person.

Do not send her photos that are sensitive. They might be considered offensive or be enticed to show them to other people or post them online.

Nobody wants to be caught in an online scandal.

If you are on dates, it is important to be careful not to text when you are talking. It's distracting, and she may think that you're not paying attention to her and are not really attracted to her. You might also believe that you constantly update your acquaintances about your date.

If you're not completely in a relationship that you are comfortable with do not discuss any sensitive issues to her.

Be sure to call her whenever you need to. There is no way to convey everything in an SMS message.

Additionally, be aware that you should not resolve any disagreement by means of texts. It is better to discuss issues in person since texts are sometimes misinterpreted.

Chapter 13: Our Final A Few Tips On How To Text A Girl

After having read the previous few chapters, you'll be able to have a good idea of how to message an attractive girl. Also, you should have some ideas regarding how you can text her during the first phases of a relationship as well as during the course of the duration of the relationship. However, I will provide a few additional tips regarding how to send a text to girls, to make sure you do the right message.

First of all, texting her should be enjoyable and should not become a chore , or that is stressful. If you discover that you're now using Google or even the Internet to get ideas for texting, you're not doing anything right. Also, it's likely that your relationship doesn't have any chance of making it through the day. Use your gut and write the way you imagine that girl would prefer to be messaged. If you've been through the article you'll already have a good EQ and a solid knowledge of the things that girls are looking for. Keep your messages light and entertaining but the most important thing is to keep your messages real. Remember that she'll love getting the type of messages you'd like to receive. Imagine your mirror-effect.

Let's review some texts that I like and which are incredibly simple and charming.

* "Hi there. I am thinking of you. Have a great day.'
* "Hiya. I recall you telling me that you'd never visited that new coffee shop that's opening on Broadway. Would you like me to give you Iced coffee?"
* "It's the first day of spring, and I want to let you know that I'm very happy, and so are you!"
* "Are you and Lola the bulldog available to go for a walk? I'm taking an hour off at work, and I would like to spend time in your company."
* "Miss you!"
* "Good morning, I'm sorry to miss you and will chat with you later. ..."
* "Sweet dreams!"

Sometimes it happens, and this is a crucial point and important to note girls get bored of texting. Everyone is bored of texting. You can lay on your couch and chat throughout the day, but eventually you are bound to become exhausted. You'll know when the right time has come to end the endless text messages and make calls. While we all hate phones nowadays however, we love getting messages from our favourite people! Therefore, at some point you might text her to write:

* "Hey. Do you want me to contact you immediately?"
* "Wouldn't it be fun to talk for a short time. Are you available? If you are, I'll contact you immediately."
* "I feel like hearing your voice. Do you mind to contact you?"

It may sound odd to verify your information prior to making a make a call, but it's actually considerate. A lot of people aren't averse to calling, in fact they love them. However, they'd like to get a caution before making a call. It's sort of a modern-day thing that you can even turn it into humorous joke.

"Okay I'm a little wary I'm about to contact you."

She'll laugh and will be thrilled to hear from you.

She'll laugh and will be thrilled to hear from you.

The other thing you should do when you text with a girl you enjoy is to make it regular. If you've been texting her each day for three days Don't stop texting her for a whole week and after that, text her. She may have lost interest in you or will believe that you're not reliable. Be consistent, particularly when you are a fan of her. If you feel that you're not a fan anymore Tell her that you've realized you aren't mutually compatible. It's always best to be truthful.

I talked about how you need to be an attentive listener. This is can be very important, and the skills of listening will help you get through the day. If you're just beginning to get to know her better, and you're apprehensive about texting allow her to take the lead. Do not do it in a way where she is forced to keep the conversation going however, show a lot of enthusiasm for what she is doing. Here are some examples.

* "Hi Rita. I'm sure you're in the field of advertising, and it's an area that has always intrigued me. Tell me about the first time you started?"

When Lesley explains more about advertising, you should show an interest. A bit similar to...

* "Wow, that's incredible. It is like a dream work. Does it?"

* "It looks like you're very proficient in your field. I would like to go through some of your work someday."

* "What do your working hours look as? I'm able to always be there to meet you in between crucial meetings, provided capable of doing that?"

Remember to take note of any anxieties or worries she might be experiencing. Although you don't want to be her therapist or an alternative to your therapist need to convey to her by text messages, that you take care of her and are a person who cares. If she messages you ensure that you've read it correctly. She might have said she's anxious about an exam scheduled to be held, or her brother is sick. Always follow-up. Here are some examples:

* "I wish you the best of luck on your test today. We'll keep you in my thoughts."

* "Write carefully and if you would like to celebrate once you've passed your test I'll be done at 5pm and would love to drink a glass of wine along with you."

* "How's your brother doing today?"

The text in these three cases shows that you are interested, and you've been paying attention.

Of course, there's one crucial aspect to all this texting. You're being courteous and kind. You're showing her you're a great listener, and that you can always stand by to help her. How does she know that you're more than just a friend? Are you flirtatious enough? Do you have to flirt in your text messages? Or do you

128

have to inform her you love her?

The most appropriate answer is yes. You should definitely be flirtatious with your messages. Also, it is a good idea to say that you are in love with her. Here are some examples of how you can be flirtatious with your messages without being too sexually explicit or crude and without scaring her away.

* "You did a great job at the event last night. I really liked your hairstyle. And your dress."
* "Do you wear red lipstick? It's very sexually attractive, I'm forced to share this with you!"
* "I was thinking I wouldn't be too excited when I message you, but, as you're aware I'm in a rush. I really like you."
* "You are aware that I smile every time your name appears within my mobile."
* "You are aware that I smile every when I think of you. I just can't stop myself."
* "Watching Friends and you're aware that you're akin to Jennifer Aniston.

Only, better! I hope that's not too silly hahaha."

If she's flirtatious when you respond to her messages You can continue the conversation. If she takes over the reins and becomes more formal, then you shouldn't try to be too aggressive. Be patient when flirting, but stay certain in your thoughts about being friend zoned. If she begins to treat you like a friend and only as an acquaintance, it's an appropriate time to remind her you really love her.

Below are some ideas on how you can send a message to someone telling them that you're interested in them.

"Would you consider this a great moment to remind you of how much I truly love you."

"You know that I consider you extremely attractive. And quite sexy!"

"Oh my goodness, I'm hoping you're not friend zoning me since I really like you quite a bit!"

"I would like to spend time with you. And in that way you know. ..."

"Your name is on my phone under very special people."

There are many ways to flirt with that beautiful hot woman, but you need to determine which one is most effective for you. Each relationship is different, and every girl, thank you also, is different. What is successful for one girl might not be the same for another, and what is successful for one guy may not work for a different guy.

Be aware of the rules to follow when texting an attractive girl to set up an opportunity to meet and have an enjoyable relationship.

"Be yourself.
* Be respectful, kind and courteous.
Don't be afraid to let your feelings be known.
* Show her you truly care about her, not just say it.
Make sure you are listening to what she says.
* Show enthusiasm for every aspect in her daily life.
Tell her about your experiences.
* Be vulnerable.
She should be open to vulnerability.
Keep things simple.
Make sure to have fun.
* Have fun and be entertaining.
* Be YOU, but be yourself.
When you're YOU everything else will be in the right

Chapter 14: The Mistakes You Should Avoid When Texting A Man

In the previous chapter we examined the secrets of sex on phones and the ways you can get your guy to go insane. In this chapter I will outline certain mistakes you should avoid when flirting with men via text and the reason why it's important to be aware of these each time you are tempted to have a chat with him.

Not Porn

If you are considering flirting, sexting, or phone sex, keep in mind that it must not be like a pornographic movie. It is not possible to watch one and then talk to your partner in the exact same manner. You should be as elegant as you can, but don't hold from expressing your sexuality. There are several ways to say the same thing. You should choose something that is stylish.

If you believe you're messaging someone who enjoys porn and demands that you speak in a casual manner, then inform him that you are not and end the texting completely. For instance: "I want you to touch my body" is more appealing than "I would like you to kiss my lips". But don't expect to tread a perfect line every single time. Once you're both comfortable with one another, you are able to utilize a bit of crude spoken language.

Don't be Obsessed

If you are looking to message him to make a flirtation do not set out on a mission to get him. It could come appearing eager or desperate to win him. You can mix your flirting with informal conversations, so that the person you are talking to won't discern the distinction. Therefore, you can flirt casually with him, rather than being direct. Only do this if you're as intrigued as you are . If you think he's not as open as you are can be, then just lie back for a bit and chat with him about everyday issues, and gradually begin to return to flirting.

Don't Be Forceful

Don't put pressure on him each time you wish to talk about something fun. Don't force him to reply to you just because you're sure he'll have the courage of answering you. These kinds of situations will not last for long, and he'll eventually become bored of your tactics. Do not take on something he's uncomfortable discussing and ask him for an opinion. If you believe the subject is dull, put it aside right away.

Respect His Mood

The way he expresses his mood is vital. If he claims it is not his intention to be at his peak, it's exactly the message he's trying to convey! Do not think that he is expecting you to speak to him to make him feel better because that's not what he's looking for. He would prefer to be on his own and if you try to force yourself onto him and try to show your love for him this could be a huge turn off for him. Respect the space he has and If you can see him asking that you should leave him alone and be quiet, do it!

Do not ever accuse

Do not claim that he did something because that could cause a major problem. If he's done something, you should say it in a fun manner , and don't use it as a way to complain. If he hasn't replied to some of your important messages don't respond with, "Hey! What's the problem? Do you not have to be a bit more responsive?" He will probably not respond following this. Instead, say, "Hey, you missed a couple of my messages. Everything is good is fine with your?" He will immediately probably respond with a pity message.

Don't be repetitive

When you are messaging men, be careful not to be monotonous and repeat the same thing repeatedly. You will appear as if you're being a little pushy and will not being as responsive as you want his response to you. Be unique and different every time , and always try to create something different. Don't bore his with the same sort of greeting each time. Try something different at the start of each new conversation.

Don't bring up Exes

As a general rule do not discuss your ex-partners never! Do not say things such as "oh I loved him, and yet the relationship ended" or "we enjoyed our relationship but everything fell apart". These types of comments are certain to make him leave for good reasons. However don't ask him about his. Women are prone to reacting too strongly to news about ex-lovers and it could create an ice between the two of you. It could cause you to be both irritable and ultimately lead to a break-up. Exes aren't a factor in your life. Even when one of you still close to them, it should not bother you one second.

Don't discuss negative experiences

Do not discuss your past relationships with your partners, particularly in the event of a negative one. Don't tell them that "Tom was a bit unsatisfying experience and I've never been satisfied however I am sure that you will". It won't be an answer for that or even a response in general! Be mindful of the words you select and avoid getting carried away. Don't talk about any topic except when absolutely essential. Don't expect it to be an effective way to inject humor because it's not.

Do not overdo any of it.

If you think that you are extremely smart, then that's something you should remain quiet about. Don'tthink you are about slamming him with fancy phrases in an attempt to show off your skills. You will be able to impress him. If you want to make it happen, then you have to do it within limitations and only when you have the circumstances to do so.

Men appreciate it when it is discreet and not overt, and they won't appreciate anything such as "hey I'm a doctor, and earn money!" $$$$$$". It appears as if you're trying to get flirty with him by showing how clever and efficient you are. Be subtle and make sure that you don't go way too far.

Don't be expecting him to come Again

If you've had a miscommunication and it's the fault of the person who made it in the whole, don't count on that he will come back to apologize. The majority of men have a huge image and aren't likely to apologize. He is not likely to return to you and say "Sorry for the fact that it wasn't your fault". He'll conclude that you've lost the interest and then move to the next. If you really love the person and want to keep him around, you should be willing to endure his antics for a time.

Then, he'll begin to sympathize with you and will not repeat your mistakes. If you're in the wrong, do not hesitate to send an apology. If it's happening on a regular basis and he's making error after another and not apology, it's ideal to let him go and switch to a different person!

Chapter 15: First Message On Dating Apps

We have mentioned the possibility of texting on mobiles. You may also have to start a conversation with a woman without a prior conversation using an online dating app or social media.

The way you communicate through these apps is the same as texting. However, it is important to be looking to obtain the girl's contact number as it is the most personal method of online communications with her.

Common mistakes

Are you getting no responses after sending a message via the application? If you do, it indicates you have several issues in your messages.

The most common errors in regards to your first messages on apps is that they're too boring, ineffective and require a lots of effort the girl to respond.

The most common messages that fail include:

* "Hey" / "Hello" / "Hi"

* "How do you feel" * "How are you "What's going on?"

These messages have already given her a negative impression of the kind of person you would be in person. It's boring, dull, and unoriginal. There's nothing in these messages that will stir enough emotion to cause her to be able to respond.

It's very passive and you're simply putting it out there in the hope of getting it to work most favorable. The message you are sending requires the most effort, that means you'll get the least amount of effort from the girl , probably zero effort. Think about what to say is the next step if she decides to respond what she could possibly say? She's likely to need to try to be interesting, as it's likely that the only thing she will be able to say is "not much" or 'I'm working or I'm watching TV' or 'I'm fine'.

There is a chance that you will get a response at times to "hey," but a girl of the highest quality you're looking for isn't going to respond because they'll have others who are sending more engaging opening messages that are more worth her time and interest.

A girl who is of high-quality on the dating app might include 3 to 5 photos of high-quality on her profile, which shows her personality and how fascinating she is. If you don't notice it, it'll look as if you're not interested in becoming acquainted with her.

How do you get the best responses?

Dating apps are awash with of users, and

girls match frequently throughout the day, which means that your message must be noticed and create positive feelings in her. There are a few ways to increase the likelihood that she'll respond to your message. We will provide some guidelines to send your first message on the internet to increase the chance of receiving a getting a response.

Method 1: Writing the story

Make a story around one of their images. Take a look at one of her photos and create a short description of what you think happens in this photo.

The secret to this method is to be funny. Don't think about it as serious. Utilize your imagination to imagine what she's up to.

Here are a few examples.

If there's a photograph of her at an Safari Park within Africa then you can write something such as:

"photo two," Sarah in a safari prior to the time she was screaming when the lions appeared".

If you have a picture of her enjoying a day at the beach it could be a good idea to write:

"photo three", Lenny as she lay in bed in the sun and had her bikini top taken".

Enjoy yourself. These are just a few examples of how to create a photo and create your own message. Use this basic idea and customize it to your personal. If you follow this method correctly you will be able to make it intriguing, and this will prompt her to want to share.

Method 2: Identifying shared ideas or experiences

It is usually performed in real-life interactions but it is effective when it comes to a dating apps as well. It's not necessary trying to create a connection "I know you like ice cream, and I too". It's too hard.

If you're not sure, try to use a phrase which shows you have the same interests , or have knowledge about an issue from personal experiences, such as "Cool that you enjoy the 'X' band. I was able to see 'X' at the 'Y' festival and they performed an incredible performance at the festival".

This has so many options to talk about without ever having to ask a query - she could tell you that she's never been to see that band live , but has always would like to, or inquire about what song you liked the most was from the evening, and so on you get the picture.

The trick to do this is to write something more specific and interesting about what you're discussing on her profile. If you can do this, she'll see that you're keen to get to know her better and realize that you have something in the same.

Method 3: Make a compliment on something she has posted about her Comment on something she discusses on her profile or on something that she is actually performing in one of her photos. There's possibly a reason for why she chose the picture. This is also a good idea since you'll be different from the others who don't have the time to have conversations with her. You could comment on the fact that she enjoys particular genres of music or even her work for money. Girls are awestruck by compliments so in the sense that they're not intrusive.

Method 4: Cold reading
Sometimes , you may not find any information from her page to discuss. In

this instance it is advisable to attempt cold reading. This is a good option when meeting women in person, so you can do it using dating apps.

It is basically trying to guess the personality of a person. People like to know what other people think about them , especially when conversations are about them. If you're speaking with a woman about yourself and she'll love responding to your questions. The best method to accomplish that is keep the conversation casual and non-insinuating.

The formula is:
1.) "Let me guessthat you're X, Z, Z. Do I have it right?
2.) "I can tell you're the girl who has X", Y, Z"

For instance:
1.) In the event that she's got a photo

showing her eating pizzas, you can use a phrase similar to "Let me guess that you're an ham and pineapple pizza person".

1.) In the event that she's got a photograph of her travels and you want to tell her something like "I know you're the type of girl who enjoys exploring" Try to be as specific to her photos as you can to ensure she is aware that you didn't just copied and pasted your words to a variety of girls. This is an original method to begin a conversation that keeps her engaged and prompt her to reply to you by commenting if you are right or not.

The general rule for increasing value
The first step in adding value to your life is sharing something fun or enjoyable with her that doesn't require any reaction from her. Here are a few

examples of what you can offer.
Funny videos or memes

One way to provide value is to send funny videos or memes. You can to create a collection of hilarious videos or memes that can text at different dates for various situations that you are able to relate to and which match your personal sense of humor. Then , you can begin sending them out in bulk.

The ability to send memes is a effective way to get started on the process of texting because they are easy to make and don't need to be personalized, which means it looks like you're not trying to difficult. They are humorous, but it also does not convey any motive. It doesn't require her to reply or to create any plans.

A personal list of photo services

Another method to increase your value is to post some intriguing personal photos you've snapped. Consider this as if likely to refresh either your profile on Facebook or Instagram by sharing a photo of your daily life that illustrates how interesting and cool you are. A photograph can tell your personality without the need to speak or boast about it.

The best thing to begin is to create an inventory of girls you've dropped contact with, or who have been silent about but are is still worthy of your attention and mass text them. There will be situations wherein a girl you believed you weren't likely to hear from is in contact with you in a flash and asking you questions such as "Where did that photo come from? What's your current location? It's adorable!" etc.

Random statements

This is the point where you begin making statements about what you observed or that happened to you. Also, you're not looking for a response through these messages. Therefore, instead of asking what she's been doing, pretend she had asked you to do that, and then simply send the message.

Naturally, if you're skilled at self-amusement and entertaining yourself, the things you share is likely to be entertaining and random. It's all about showing her humorous things you've noticed and you can discuss the events that you've observed without filtering. For instance, you can tell a funny story you witnessed, for instance "just witnessed Joker enter my bank, I'm expecting an imminent robbery" or "just observed a man being hit by a bird, not so fortunate! ".

Therefore, you must share things that you find humorous or interesting as it can demonstrate your personality which is appealing to women. If you're having fun and having a great time, she'll be delighted.

Therefore, your aim is to convey your expertise quickly and easily to a variety of people. You're not seeking anything or to receive any response or any other way. You're trying to create excitement, so when she gets an SMS message from you the first thing she thinks is that it's going be something that will be exciting and enjoyable. Once you've begun a conversation, you're able to move forward and move on to the next stage of demonstrating your worth.

To make a woman interested in you she's

likely to perceive you as a high-value person. If you are perceived as an attractive person, you'll enjoy many advantages, as she's more likely to say yes to your demands and may even pursue you. There are ways to show your worthiness by sub-labeling your text messages.

Abundance vs Neediness

One of the biggest mistakes when it comes to texting is appearing insecure and desperate.

You'll be perceived as needy If you do not respond promptly constantly. For instance, if you text and the girl takes an entire day to respond and then you respond within a minute, and it takes two days to get her reply, and you reply within a minute, this will make you appear unimportant since you've got nothing else to do.

Therefore, unless you're in a straight back and forth conversation don't respond immediately. If you cannot do that, then at a minimum give yourself five minutes so that you don't appear as if you're sitting at your phone, waiting for her text messages all day long.

If you're wealthy this means that you're doing your thing and have no time to text your girl and you've got several women around you. If you're blessed by your mentality, then you don't be too concerned about particular text message because there are plenty of options. Therefore, the most effective way to feel rich is to text many girls simultaneously since you're not tied to one particular conversation.

Over texting

Before sending a text consider asking yourself what you intend to accomplish with the text? Each text should have a goal or a message for it. If, for instance, you're like me and doing great How have you been? What are you doing? You are planning to have a drink on Saturday? This is three texts in one. The messages that attempt to accomplish more than they can accomplish come across as demanding and impatient. In this case the message should be simple and concise.

The choice to not reply to texts

One of the mistakes that men do is to feel the need to respond to everything she has said. There are occasions where there's no need for sending a message. A text that is meaningless may not cause any harm, but it's not doing anything , and it's not helping the situation.

In some situations, it's more appropriate that she text you last , and you didn't reply back. If you don't respond in some cases it can make her think she made a mistake or sent an inappropriate text, which will cause her to become more interested. Be aware of these opportunities.

It is a good idea to organize details or the text is generally requiring an answer or you're having an enjoyable, good back-andforth dialogue and are getting closer to the girl, you must continue texting. But, if you feel that the conversation isn't going anywhere and you're able to let it go You should take this chance to let her know that you want her to be a little. The reason guys need to be responsive to every situation is that they're afraid that if they don't respond and the lady doesn't respond, then they're not sure how to add value down the road. This is a low value behavior. Do not be concerned about it and believe that you're capable of providing value at any moment or even reply to the same issue after six hours. If you've achieved at that point what you wanted to accomplish The best message you can offer is silence, and then use the situation to gain.

Calibration

To be attractive to the girl you'll need to figure out what she considers attractive whether it is physical characteristics like status or connections? When you text, if you realize that she puts physical attributes as top of their list, then may like to send her some pictures of you working out at the gym. If she is a fan of status, then you may like to let her know that you spend a lot of traveling. The idea of traveling is usually associated with an inflated value as the majority of people work from 9 to 5 and have little of time to travel.

The possibility that you travel and taking nice photos is a sign that you're worth it. If you believe that she is a person who values connection and connection, then you may prefer spending more time in discussing your hopes and feelings, as well as your goals and your spirituality. It is important to make sure to show that you meet the criteria for her to have a conversation with you.

Chapter 16: How Soon Do I Text Her

The rule of three days is a good one in regards to texting her. Not enough to make it appear as though you're desperate, but lengthy enough to ensure that she doesn't seem to forget your name. If you're getting her phone number , it's recommended to choose her some sort of nickname. It doesn't need to be complicated. punk, shorty, risk and pixie are all acceptable.

If you want to text her you can use her name within your message. The benefit of the method is that it doesn't need to begin your text by saying "Hey This is Toby." Simply use the name you used to call her, and it'll be immediately clear that you're who you say you are. If the woman you're messaging is attractive it isn't necessary to assume that you're the only person who has her number.

Another suggestion is to text her immediately after you have her number. You can do this by sending a message that says "like I'm not checking you in." This helps make certain that you've received her actual phone number and shows that you're confident and a fun person.

One message you shouldn't write is "It was really wonderful to get to know the two of you" text. A lot of guys who have had the pleasure of meeting someone nice will find that they're eager to share the wonderful encounter was with her. Although the gesture is sweet and genuine, it also makes appear desperate. You just have to wait until the period of three days to come completed and then text her.

Like everything else, the three day rule is designed to be violated. People who have experience with seduction are often able to be able to text earlier because their game of texting is so easy. For the majority of guys, it's best to wait until three days have expired.

What should you do when she won't
If she does not respond to you following your initial message Sorry buddy, but you're lost. Women don't have an obligation to join you, and should she not want to respond, it's time to go on. It is important to realize the fact that simply because she provided you her number does not necessarily mean that she's interested in continuing to talk. There could be a relationship with a man who has ended a relationship, have just been reunited or she may not be a fan of you. Let it be and go on with your life. The act of sending another text message is getting into stalker territory, and isn't a

great location for her or the other person to end up. Although it may sound corny, it's true that there are plenty more fish in the ocean.

Problems with texting

Texting can be a fantastic method to connect with women and establish friendship. But it does have negatives, and by being aware of these will make it easier to avoid falling into common traps.

Moving Slowly and Nowhere

Moving slowly and in a slow manner is a trap some men slip into when messaging a girl. You could have been messaging for months or even weeks without ever getting together in person. I've observed that this issue is most prevalent with people who have connected through a dating site. They've managed to obtain her phone number, but due to any reason, they are unable to take her to go out for an evening date.

It's usually due to two reasons. It could be that it is the woman who is in a state of evasion. It is the time when you've attempted to propose an opportunity to meet, but she always gives a reason as to why she won't but she is still able to message you. If you've been communicating for months or even weeks without meeting for a face-to-face date, then it's unlikely to take place. The woman might never be telling you that makes her feel like she's got a boyfriend or perhaps she appreciates the attraction more than the thought of a relationship. Women who've been hurt in their last relationships may be in a situation in which they desire to feel loved but aren't quite ready to start a new one. However, when they do feel at ease and ready to begin her new relationship, it's not with one of the guys whom she's been texting for the last few months while she was healing her heart. A new person will appear when the time is right and your texting conversations will come to an close. If you're in this scenario, it doesn't necessarily mean you need to stop communicating with her. It is possible to use texting to practice, and there's a slight chance that it could be a way to get somewhere. However, you must make an honest assessment of the situation, however, and recognize that it's probably won't be the case and that you should be contacting other women.

The second scenario is where you've been unable to pull the trigger , and you ask her out. You are likely to have come up with a reason within your head for as to why you haven't gotten her out to date yet. You may think that this isn't the best moment or that you prefer to slow things down. This is a method to justify your own anxieties. You're scared of losing the friendship you've made, so you aren't willing to take a an opportunity to request her to meet. However, the longer you keep messaging without asking her out, the further into the realm of friends you'll be. It is the place where she will see her as an acquaintance more than a possible lover. Once you're there, it's difficult to break away from the situation.

If you try to approach her there's no doubt an opportunity that she might not like the request but until you decide to move, you're not going to be able to tell. The longer you are waiting, the more likely to be that she'll tell you that she will not.

Turning Her into Your Dream Girl

This is a frequent issue for those who

only met online, but it can also happen when texting too. It is the case when you appear to be in a great relationship with the girl is texting you, yet you haven't had the chance to meet her in person yet. Based on what you've learned about her, she appears to be the ideal woman and checks every box. However, what you must know is that she most likely, it has to be more a result of an image you've imagined in your head rather than the actual facts of who she really is.

If we don't know who someone is, it's simple to fill in blanks by using the information we have. We tend to think of them as ideal because we believe that our minds are capable of filling in the gaps with the information we imagine she'll be. We haven't even had the pleasure of meeting her, we've not been confronted with the flaws she could have.

If the concept of the dream girl can blossom, we could eventually grow her to the size of a king. Even though we've never seen her, it is still true love. It is true that affection is when you feel you love someone in all aspects of who they are. This will only happen once you have met them. This is the reason why you must try to get into a face-to-face meeting as soon as you can so that you can figure out if the real you is actually meeting your expectations. If you discover that she isn't eager to meet you , for whatever reason, don't be a victim of the notion that she could have been the perfect woman for you. If you had met her, she probably wouldn't have live up to the image of a woman you imagined in your head.

Don't confuse texting with reality. Texting is a fantastic method of building sexual tension and arousal that could spill over into real life once you get together. But , at the same time, you must ensure that you're not muddled in how you communicate with your real-life counterparts.

Whatever flirtatious texts may be, until you actually meet you won't be able to tell if they are real. If you are able to text correctly, it can help build sexual tension so that , when you do meet , you are able to quickly advance the conversation. However, remember that flirting with text messages is not the relationship itself.

Communication is easy

Texting can be a source of confusion because of two reasons. It is the first reason that we don't have any body language to refer to, therefore it's easy to interpret things wrong. We can tell when someone is playing with us by the expression at their face. But without these visual clues, it's easy to conclude that they're just doing it to be mean. If the way women typically communicate does not translate well into text, it could be due to this issue.

One way to solve this issue is by using emoticons. Emoticons and phrases like LOL can play the same function as the body language we use in everyday life. While some men may be unwilling to use them due to the fact that they do not want to be perceived in the same way as a 16 year old, they play a crucial role in the process of communicating via text. If you are concerned that the words you're using could be misinterpreted, use emoticons;) to reduce the impact.

Also, men and women communicate differently, so when we text, it's possible for her to view your messages in a different way. When you text, examine the way you communicate and remain in tune with her style. It is best to keep your messages short If she is an elongated writing style, you shouldn't send out only just one word responses. It's simple for her to see this as rude.

It Provides a Permanent Record

If you have sent something out via text, it's pretty difficult to retake (Although Tiger Text does overcome some of these issues). This is why it is important be thinking about your message before you hit send. Although you shouldn't overthink your messaging game in the end, dating is supposed to be enjoyable. It is important to ensure that prior to you claim that she is cheating, that it is the message you intend to send. Once you have put it out there, it's not going to come back and unlike conversation, in which you could pretend that she was misunderstood, or in any other way get from the situation you've put yourself in, it's much more difficult to do this when you text.

Another issue the friend of ours Tiger Woods discovered, is that if you're with several girls and you'd prefer that one did not find out about text messages, they can provide indisputable proof of your cheating methods. If you're in this scenario, be sure to delete your messages and verify your messages right away before others do.

Chapter 17: Sexting The Right Way

Like any other activity or display there are rules to follow for appropriate etiquette. There are rules to be followed when you're looking to flirt with someone. In this chapter , you're going to be taught what are the "dos" as well as the "don'ts" of sexting.

Modern technology has shaped our society and there are few people who do not have a mobile phone and even fewer doesn't know how to send a text message. Go up a notch and ask yourself how many people aged between 18 and 50 who not sent their loved ones an unsolicited text message. The majority of people are aware of this type of foreplay.

While having fun aside, it's important to be aware that sexting can be risky when it is not done in a appropriate manner and with the correct person. It could end up being harmful or even ruin different aspects of your life. And to address the question that's in heated debate, yes dating someone is not a part of your life and being taken with to be doing a prank. It's a kind of foreplay.

Dos and Don'ts Dos

Begin Slowly

There's no rush in foreplay. Therefore, be patient when it comes to sexual sexting. It's an individual kind of game and we are aware that foreplay that is rushed is not good. It's a way to build anticipation. Make sure to tease and teasing however, save the best sections for later when you have a conversation. It's never a regret to go this way.

You can play with a person You Cred
It's not a smart option to engage in sexting with someone you've not seen naked before or just had a brief conversation with. Sexting should be something that's shared by you and a person you trust. In the absence of trust, you can't blame anyone else if your inappropriate photos end up in the inboxes and messages of people who you know.

Sext If You Are Not Together
It doesn't matter if you're out for the night because of an obligation or going on business it is a fantastic way to keep that flame bright red while you're absent. Let your partner know that you're thinking of them, and imagine

what the next reunion might be like.

Remember to press Delete

It's fun to go back and review the messages, but if your phone gets snatched up by a curious snoop, the fun has ended. Be sure to delete the conversation after it's over. Delete, delete, delete!

Utilize Auto Correct

A message packed with misspellings can be an absolute turn-off. It's embarrassing and the person who reads it is likely to shrug off your message quickly. If you're not sure the correct spelling of an word, do not use it. You can substitute the word or use auto correct to make you appear more knowledgeable.

The Don'ts

Sexting with someone unknown
Don't sext anyone who you haven't seen
naked. This can result in an awkward
and, often, a threatening scenario.
Engage in conversation and save photos
for later within the relationships. For
men The girl doesn't want to see pictures
of your genitals. Make her feel sexy
instead.

Do Things You Wouldn't Say in Person to
Someone
The best part about sexting is that you
can't look at the face of the person.
There is nothing to worry about. But, it
could get back on your face if your
spouse asks you to speak it out during
the event. This means that if you send it,

you must be able to express it in the presence of a person.

Utilize a Work Phone

Personal messages must always be made available via your personal phone. There are always risks and accidents that could result in losing your job. It's common sense; but, it's been a frequent occurrence.

Send the pictures using Your Face

Do not send photos that display your face or other characteristic that is visible to the naked eye. If something happens where the photo is seen, no one would know it's you.

Don't forget the age limit

Do not forget that sexting can be an 18 year old or older kind of activity. If both or one of them are doing it, it's not right and must stop immediately.

Hunt for Numbers Social Media
Don't try to find the phone number of someone you saw on social media and then sext them. You should have a chat first. The person needs to get acquainted with you. And let's admit it is a little stalkerish when you try to track their number but they don't give the information to you. Legal action could be taken if this occurs.

Ask for pictures
If you don't have any personal contact with them and you aren't in a relation with them, don't request "boob" images.

A lot of women get these requests , and it can make them mad. You will never get the images, so do not do it.

Type Orgasms

It's awkward and rude to send a text message with an orgasm. Avoid sending "ooooh" as well as "aaauuggh". It's considered foolish. In addition, how can you feel a gasp when typing?

Conclusion

Before you leave I'd like you thank you for your purchase "thank to you" for buying this eBook.

I'm sure that you could have picked one of several books on relationships and dating. However, you decided to rely on my book.

Also, I would like to offer my sincere thank you for taking the time to download this book and then going through it to the very end!

If you enjoyed the book, I ask you to write a brief review on Amazon to let others go through it. Your feedback will allow me to write other books about the mysterious nature of relationships between females and males.

CPSIA information can be obtained
at www.ICGtesting.com
Printed in the USA
LVHW081605261222
735894LV00014B/785